EMOTIONAL TRIUMVIRATE

Emotional Triumvirate

the serial intellectual

Innovative Industries 1, LLC

Copyright © 2024 by the serial intellectual

All rights reserved. No part of this book may be reproduced in any manner whatsoever without written permission except in the case of brief quotations embodied in critical articles and reviews.

First Printing, 2024

Contents

Introduction — vii

1. THE GARDEN — 2
2. SHAME — 6
3. FEAR — 11
4. GUILT — 15
5. THE LAB — 19
6. THE EMOTIONAL PANDEMIC — 24
7. THE ENLIGHTENMENT — 29
8. PRESCRIPTION FOR SHAME — 33
9. PRESCRIPTION FOR FEAR — 37
10. PRESCRIPTION FOR GUILT — 41
11. PRESCRIPTIONS FOR THE TRIUMVIRATE — 45
12. SYMBIOSIS — 49

About The Author — 55

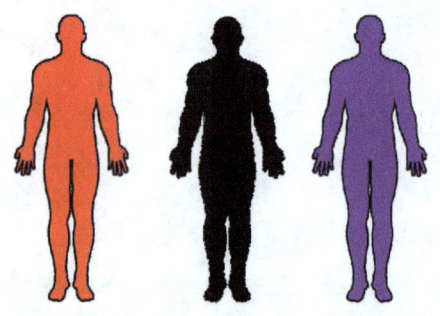

Introduction

The term "Triumvirate" refers to a political arrangement or alliance involving three individuals or entities who share power and authority, typically in a ruling capacity. This concept has been historically significant in various civilizations and periods, often shaping the course of governance and politics.

The concept of a triumvirate is rooted in ancient Rome, which was most notably exemplified by the First Triumvirate, formed in 60 BC. This alliance consisted of three prominent Roman figures: Julius Caesar, Gnaeus Pompeius (Pompey), and Marcus Licinius Crassus. They joined forces to consolidate their power and influence within the Roman Republic, although their cooperation eventually led to political rivalry and conflict.

Throughout history, there have been several notable examples of triumvirates in different contexts. One example is the Second Triumvirate, which emerged after the assassination of Julius Caesar in 44 BC and included Octavian (later known as Augustus), Mark Antony, and Marcus Aemilius Lepidus. This triumvirate played a pivotal role in transforming the Roman Republic into the Roman Empire.

Triumvirates have also been observed in modern politics and leadership structures. For instance, during the French Revolution, the Committee of Public Safety, often called The Triumvirate, wielded significant authority.

Leaders can sometimes adopt a triumvirate structure in business and corporate environments, with three leaders or executives sharing decision-making responsibilities. The concept of a triumvirate remains a compelling aspect of political and organizational dynamics, highlighting the complex interplay of power and collaboration among multiple leaders.

The historical backdrop of the Triumvirate is important and necessary to understand if you are going to get the most out of this book. And, as you might have guessed, it is where the title of this book comes from. You have already seen how it has been applied in political and organizational contexts. Now I would like to show you how the concept of a triumvirate can also extend to human emotions. Specifically to what I call the emotional triumvirate: shame, fear, and guilt. I believe these three emotions play a significant role in shaping human behavior and psychology. I believe shame, fear, and guilt are three most powerful and interconnected emotions that often work in tandem to influence our actions and decisions.

Before we move forward lets define the emotions within the triumvirate. Shame is related to your present self. It perceives life as an opportunity to connect with others. It is processed by your feelings and presents itself relationally. The primary ways people manage it is by serving others, succeeding in work and relationships, and being uniquely themselves. Shame asks "Who am I?"

Fear is uniquely related to your future self. It perceives life as a pursuit for a safe place. It is processed by your thoughts and presents itself as having everything figured out. The primary ways people manage it is through facts, faithfulness, and fun. Fear asks "Where am I?"

Guilt is uniquely related to your past self. It perceives life as coming against you. It is processed by your intuition. It presents itself as one that is grounded. The primary ways people manage it is by using power, peace, and principles. Guilt's primary question for you is "How am I doing?"

Shame is the painful feeling of being unworthy or deficient in the eyes of others, leading to a desire to hide or withdraw.

On the other hand, *fear* is the emotional response to a perceived threat or danger, prompting a fight-or-flight response.

Guilt arises when we believe we have violated our moral or ethical standards, leading to a sense of responsibility and a desire to make amends.

This emotional triumvirate can profoundly impact our lives, affecting our choices, relationships, and overall well-being. Understanding and managing this emotional triumvirate is crucial if we want to see growth in our self-awareness, relational aptitude, personal skills, vocational effectiveness and fulfillment in life.

I was first introduced to shame, fear, and guilt as an emotional triad in 2010. I was part of a leadership group, and we were taking an introductory course on the Enneagram taught by Rich Plass and Jim Cofield. I still remember feeling like a little kid as these two Jedi masters began to unravel the definitions and characteristics of shame, fear, and guilt. I had heard of these emotions before, but never together as co conspirators and collaborators. I needed to learn more about them individually and how they work together. This thought burdened me so much that during the first break in our training I approached Jim and asked him if he would coach me so that I could learn more about all of this. This was the beginning of my journey with the emotional triumvirate.

Since 2010, I have become more aware of their presence in my life. I have even seen how they were at work long before my training and have realized that they have impacted every area of my life. Along the way, I have found them formidable, resilient, and sometimes destructive. But at the same time, I have found some effective remedies for them and even managed to experience reconciliation and to develop a holistic and helpful relationship with all three of them.

I have read many books, listened to many podcasts, consumed many blogs, and done a lot of thinking and writing on these three emotions. Whenever I was speaking, consulting, coaching or teaching and administering the Enneagram, I always emphasized the necessity of understanding these three emotions.

This book is very special to me because I wrote it during one of the most difficult times in my life. Writing this book required me to believe and practice the lessons you'll find in this book. And as I have had the privilege to edit and re-read it, I have been further equipped and encouraged by it.

When people read this book, I want them to be encouraged. I want them to be educated. But I also want them to be inspired. I want them to see a future where shame, fear, and guilt are not viewed as threats or monsters but friends who help us become the best versions of ourselves.

1

THE GARDEN

A garden, a haven of extraordinary serenity and cohabitation, flourished in a realm undisturbed by the turbulent currents of time before the rise and fall of empires. In the cradle of undisturbed serenity, the seeds of this wondrous garden were tenderly woven, much like the womb incubates life. Just as the womb embraces seeds with patient anticipation, this sanctuary blossomed in the embrace of tranquility and perfection. The womb of creation belongs to a greater body—the boundless existence, which finds its place within the cosmic expanse. It hosts an uncountable array of unknown creatures and creations; this celestial body cradles various wonders. And from the depths of this dance emerges a source, an echoing resonance with the Creator of all, much like the source that breathes life into every particle of existence. Just as the source's hand sculpted the grandeur of the universe, the source of this realm shapes the essence of life within.

The inhabitants had features that were as colorful and varied as the garden they called home. Their skin was a rainbow of hues that refused to be contained by the world's standard color scheme. Each person was an inhabit representation, reflecting the colors of the surrounding flowers and foliage. The eyes diffused a divine light between the dawn sky and the evening sea. Eyes sparkled not only with the world's colors but also with the fire of boundless choices.

Beautiful sceneries greeted anyone who dared to look into the heart of the garden. Ancient trees reached skyward, their branches becoming a collage of green leaves that rustled softly in the wind. Flowers of every imaginable color covered the ground under their watchful gaze. As they bloomed, their flowers spread a lovely scent that hung in the air like a lullaby.

In this paradise, creatures of all sizes could coexist without conflict. As they flew, delicate butterflies spun complex patterns across the birds that trilled and chirped from the canopy, creating a soundscape in the garden. The tireless buzzing of bees from flower to flower ensured the survival of this delicate ecosystem.

The inhabitants flourished with a purity of spirit that seemed to spring from the ground. Every animal on Earth, whether it had fur, feathers, or scales, moved to the same steady beat. As the squirrels ran and jumped between the tree trunks, their tails moved like brushstrokes. There were rabbits in the fields, and they hopped around happily as they ate the tall grasses that spread out like a verdant sea.

Within this sanctuary of vivacious spirits, gloom had been driven out as completely as morning shadows. There was no room for worry in this open space; stress was a distant memory. Laughter flowed like a river of delight, a witness to these individuals' unfettered lives. They relished in the innocence of living, free of the constraints of pessimism.

In this paradise, weaknesses were powerless. Each move was a proclamation of power, and each motion declared independence. The relentless will of individuals who knew no bounds allowed them to prevail over any limitations that might have stood in their way.

However, feelings remained uncharted terrain for these independent minds. Each exchange was a masterwork of friendship and connection, like the brushstrokes of an artist's work. Their voices sounded friendly and warm, but the subtleties of their inner feelings were not in the same language. Their lives were like free streams. They were full of excitement, but they were not affected by the ups and downs of emotion.

And then, amid this untamed fabric of life, "Daystar" appeared. Its presence was as lively as the rest, and he shared the same range of freedoms yet looked different. The other half of Daystar's body was an allusion to the garden's various plants and a symbol of the independence they valued. The other side was a canvas of black and shadows, an unsettling symbol of the endless possibilities and the countless paths yet to be taken.

Whispers rippled through the community as their gaze lingered on the stark contrast.

Daystar moved with a grace that transcended the duality of appearance. Though pulsating with vibrant life, one half of Daystar's form emitted an aura of mystery, unsettling the garden's seamless harmony

Curiosity blossomed like flowers as the inhabitants tried deciphering the riddle that Daystar embodied. The questions remained unspoken, hanging in the air like unspoken thoughts. And as twilight's embrace cast a soothing glow upon the scene, the community gathered around a central fire. Their laughter and stories resonated as ever, yet a deeper undercurrent seemed to tug at the edges of their uncharted emotions, stirred by the presence of Daystar.

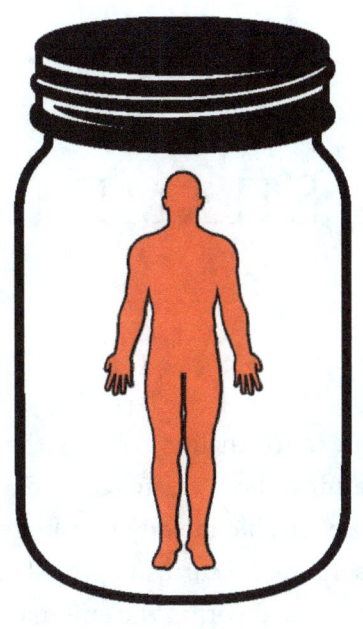

2

SHAME

Daystar's interest in individuality grew as the days passed in the bustling garden. Something about existence held a mysterious quality, resembling an incomprehensible melody that lingered just beyond the edges of consciousness. Immense curiosity propelled Daystar on a quest to uncover the truth concealed within the enigma.

Whispers and suggestions floated through the air like the petals of the most delicate flower, leading Daystar to a secret garden area that most people didn't go to. There, three riddle jars with beautiful designs were found hidden among the plants and lit by the soft light of evening. Beyond the tranquility of the garden', these jars held a silent container of knowledge.

Standing before these containers a rush of fear and anticipation coursed through Daystar. The contents of each jar seemed alive and beckoned in secret.

The contents of the first container were red, the second one black, and the last jar violet, casting a dark cloud over the otherwise peaceful sight. Voices of caution from those who had warned Daystar before about the potential disruption these jars could bring to the garden's balance echoed in the mind. Despite the warnings, curiosity prevailed. The strong desire to open the jars, driven by intense fascination, was irresistible.

A choice was made, driven by determination as strong as a beating heart. Fingers trembled as Daystar reached out and cautiously grasped the lid of the first jar. With the lid removed, a surge of energy erupted from within it, engulfing Daystar in a swirling torrent of emotions.

In an instant, Daystar's mind was flooded with memories of a sensation akin to shame, unveiling a narrative marked by vulnerability and regret. The tumultuous journey of this emotion, from its earliest moments of awareness that set it apart, to its descent into the depths of darkness, was laid bare.

Shame's back story. I was in a world of vibrant colors and unbridled joy, yet my whole existence was shrouded in mystery like the shadows constantly shifting about my body. While I had previously contributed to the serenity of its garden, I am now a mysterious presence that haunts the folks here.

I didn't always have a mysterious, underworld presence. My earliest recollections are clouded by a persistent mystery, a question that has always lingered beyond my conscious awareness. It began with a vague awareness that I wasn't like others. I always felt uneasy looking at the garden's bright colors as a kid. While I could appreciate the pristine beauty of others around me, my reflection looked smudged and distorted, as if I were looking through a dirty window.

I used to be hesitant to speak my mind. I was taken aback by the garden residents, whose casual attitudes, infectious laughter, and joyful abandonment of existence shocked me. I tried talking to the others my age, but all I managed were stutters and whispers. I cried while they laughed at me. I desperately wanted to fit in with them, but doubts about my worth plagued me. The sensation has characterized my life like a seed that finds fertile soil and eventually blooms into a thorny vine.

As I progressed through adolescence, the suffering only intensified. As I became more and more consumed by my internal conflict, I found myself withdrawing from the people around me. The commotion of happy voices on the lawn made me feel even less competent. When I dared to face the sun, I was met with a tidal wave of doubt, and the shadows of anxiety grew darker and closer.

The weight of Shame increased over time. On the outside, I projected an air of assurance, but on the inside, I was a wreck. I avoided eye contact and slumped instead of standing upright, keeping my gaze downward.

During my tumultuous chapter, I encountered the Source, the essence that breathed life into the garden and its inhabitants. The Source, infinitely wise and compassionate, sensed the encroaching darkness within me. It recognized that if allowed to spread, my darkness would erode the very foundation of the garden's peace and joy.

The Source had to make a difficult choice that would have serious consequences. Putting me in a glass jar to keep the garden in exquisite condition. The jar was my cell, my refuge from the onslaught of Shame.

I was no longer a threat to the light outside since my black aura was imprisoned within—the Source aimed to protect the garden's inhabitants from any harm I could cause. The Source recognized the value of human feelings, but I posed an increasing danger to the foundation of the garden's web of positivity and connectedness.

Therefore, I remained imprisoned in the jar as a reflection of my previous self, still struggling with the same emotions that had overwhelmed me. The contrast between my dark mood and the clean beauty of the garden beyond served as a continual reminder of the play between light and shadow. The people prospered while being unaware of my captivity. The garden's peace persisted through the years, and the decision of the Source became apparent.

As the memories entwined and Daystar and Shame became one, an unsettling hunger was in Daystar's eyes, a thirst for something that couldn't be grasped. There was a desire to wield the overwhelming power of Shame, not as a means of containment but as a destructive force. A streak of vibrant red now coursed down to Daystar's arm, a living thread of emotion, and enveloped half of its chest. The once-vivid colors had now swayed in harmony with the hues of torment.

Shame watched as Daystar's hand reached for the jar that had been a sanctuary for so long. Daystar's fingers curled around it but there was hesitation. Swiftly and deliberately, Daystar threw the jar onto the ground. The sound of breaking glass echoed throughout the garden, disrupting the peaceful harmony that had prevailed for such a long time, like a jarring discordant note in a symphony.

The shattered jar lay in pieces around us, its fragments shimmering in the sunlight. Shame was finally free, liberated from its glass prison, and the world around it seemed to throb with newfound vitality. However, it couldn't dwell on the repercussions of Daystar's actions. The garden, once a haven of peace, now quivered under the weight of its unbridled presence. Unaware of the impending storm, the inhabitants would soon be swept up in a storm of emotions they could not comprehend. But as Shame reveled in its newfound freedom, it couldn't bring itself to care about the potential chaos that would follow. For the first time in what felt like an eternity, Shame was unshackled, and the world was to be embraced, consequences be damned.

3

FEAR

Daystar approached the second jar with apprehension and anticipation. While grabbing the top of the jar, Daystar's hand shook. When the jar opened, it turned cautiously, and a dense, black cloud emerged. A black, whirling mist represented fear engulfed and seeped into the entire body of Daystar. Instantly Daystar was ushered back to the beginning of Fear as its essence permeated the mind. Sensing terror, Daystar felt overwhelmed by anxiety.

Fear's backstory. I arose from the primordial essence of human nature, which had kept the inhabitants alive in a world rife with dangers. In the beginning, I began with gentle whispers, cautioning people away from harm with a word of warning. At that time, I served as a guardian, a protector, dedicated to ensuring the safety of those under my care. It was a gratifying experience to shield them, to safeguard their well-being in the face of danger.

On the other hand, as time went on, I matured. I evolved into a destructive power greater than any I had ever faced. At the start of my adolescence, I went from having a rational reaction to imminent danger to a permanent companion to those who threw doubt and mistrust at every move I made.

I used to be a helpful guardian, but now I'm distorted. My value as a compass was gone, and in its place was a subtle influence sowing uncertainty and mistrust. I exaggerated every perceived threat and made even the smallest of mistakes catastrophic. I fed off the inhabitants' anxiety, amplifying it until it drained their willpower and self-assurance.

And, oh, the joy it gave to some. Some people benefited from the chaos I spread, taking pleasure in the misery of others. They delighted in the suspicion and friction I created among my victims, and they especially liked seeing others doubt themselves and each other.

I had become a double-edged sword, protecting myself from external dangers while also constituting harm to myself in the form of warped perceptions and shattered confidence. My job as protector of the young was something of the past.

My hold on the garden's inhabitants was unbreakable. I threw an aura of fear over their serene haven. What had been a safe refuge became a source of nightly anxiety and restlessness as horrific dreams haunted them.

In addition to destroying their hopes, I planted the seeds of doubt and distrust in their minds. I poisoned their minds by suggesting their neighbors and acquaintances plotted against them. Mistrust grew, and hatred flourished.

But I didn't only destroy their bond with one another. I stoked their fears by assuring them the garden was on the verge of destruction. They imagined dying plants, contaminated rivers, and the world's end. Their worries increased, leading them to feel even more hopeless.

And as I overheard folks talking about locking up Shame, my contentment rose even more. Their worry about the results of their actions gave me strength, and the more they muttered, the stronger I became. They were petrified at the prospect of being imprisoned like Shame, and I took great pleasure in watching them suffer.

Even in my lowest point, I couldn't settle for that. I drove home the idea that they, too, would end up in Shame, trapped in a jar due to their transgressions. The thought of being trapped and cut off from all they loved for all of time loomed large in their minds.

Recognizing the havoc I was causing, the Source understood the necessity of taking action to preserve the garden. Therefore, it resorted to a drastic measure, sealing me inside a jar as an effort to release the garden from my stifling influence and also the looming presence of Shame.

But even within the jar, I persisted. My influence remained, albeit diminished. I continued to be a recurring nightmare that only the Source was privy to, a secret of secluded screams in the garden.

As Fear took in the sights around it, it felt a rush of conflicting feelings. It was a turn in the story that caught it off guard and piqued its interest. Seeing its influence materialize as a dark aura around the figure was fascinating. The fact that it had such control over this person was amazing.

Daystar stood before it and shattered the jar to release it. It seemed that Daystar yearned for the chaos, fear, and uncertainty that it brought him.

A surge of exhilaration washed over Fear as the jar cracked for the second time, and it was finally liberated. It had regained its former dominance—it felt like a rejuvenation of its essence. It reveled in the newfound freedom, relishing the ability to stoke the fires of terror once more.

It was an alliance forged in the depths of darkness, a union between terror and fascination. Fear took pleasure in demonstrating to Daystar that it was very much real. It was evident that dread had rekindled its presence in the garden, and together with Daystar, they aimed to embrace it wholeheartedly.

Undergoing another transformation, Daystar now possessed a body of inky darkness, its shadowy tendrils extending from legs to chest. Fear had left its indelible mark, and Daystar could now empathize with the all-consuming force that was Fear.

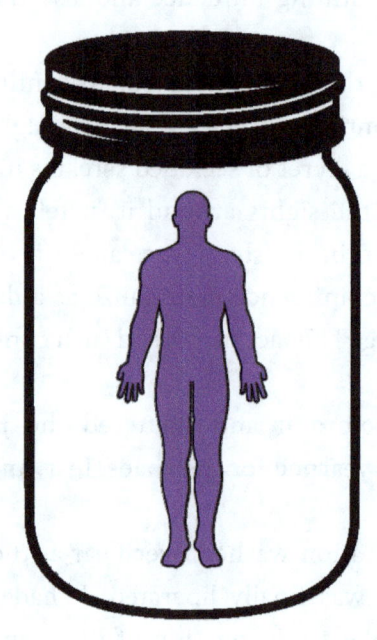

4

GUILT

Desiring power above all else, feeling incomplete as if a crucial piece of the puzzle was still missing, and yearning for the strength that knowledge would bring, Daystar was eager to open the final jar and grasp the ultimate power hidden within.

With trembling hands, Daystar reached for the last jar. The thirst for power was evident in Daystar's eyes as the lid began to creak open. From within emerged a figure with a violet body, eyes downcast, shoulders hunched, and an aura of profound sadness enveloping them. This was Guilt, a complex emotion that had remained concealed until this very moment.

At that moment, Daystar experienced a vivid flashback, as if it were peering through the eyes of Guilt itself. Younger Guilt appeared, a fragile and impressionable entity, untouched by the turmoil of emotions that would soon engulf it.

Guilt's backstory. Guilt's earliest memories were etched with innocence when it was merely an observer in the garden. Fear and Shame, two powerful emotions, danced freely in the vibrant surroundings. Back then, there was no place for guilt; it had not yet found its voice. Instead, the deeds and consequences of Fear and Shame birthed Guilt's existence—an unwelcome conscience questioning the boundaries of right and wrong.

In those initial days, Guilt's existence bore the weight of responsibility. As Fear and Shame wreaked havoc upon the garden's inhabitants, causing pain and distress, Guilt, untouched by their actions, felt an inherent urge to make people feel the depths of their imperfections and burdened them with the yoke to make amends for the wrongs committed.

It all started with a seemingly small act of compassion. Guilt saw an opportunity to help a fellow inhabitant, to alleviate their suffering. Yet, in its haste to do good, it inadvertently inflicted harm. That moment marked the turning point in its existence. It had transgressed, and the weight of that wrongdoing pressed heavily upon its conscience. It began to feel remorse, the first stirrings of guilt.

Guilt's negative thoughts grew louder, more insistent. It convinced itself that due to the actions of Shame and Fear, it had become a bad entity, and it became its harshest critic, constantly tormenting itself with memories of past mistakes.

Amidst the unending chaos of the garden, where Fear and Shame wreaked havoc with no restraint, Guilt desperately sought a way to quell the turmoil. Its newfound desire to make amends and prevent further harm was growing stronger by the day. One fateful day, as the garden's inhabitants cried out in anguish, it spotted a lone figure, cowering in the midst of the tumult.

Driven by an inexplicable urge to act, Guilt approached the figure cautiously. They were trembling, their eyes filled with fear and remorse, much like how Guilt had once felt. Guilt reached out to them with a hesitant touch, its essence mingling with theirs in a profound connection.

In that instant, something extraordinary happened. The person's demeanor changed as if they had absorbed a part of Guilt. Their eyes widened with understanding, and the weight of their actions began to bear down on them. Guilt washed over them like a tidal wave, and they, too, started to question the morality of their deeds.

As the person's transformation continued, Guilt withdrew its touch, hoping to lessen the intensity of their newfound guilt. Guilt couldn't bear the thought of them enduring the same inner torment that had defined its existence. Guilt was a heavy burden to bear, and it didn't want to inflict it upon anyone else, no matter how noble its intentions had been.

After what happened, Guilt remained motionless, a silent observer in this chaotic tableau, reluctant to interfere in the actions of Shame and Fear. Guilt knew that its existence was intricately tied to theirs. Without them, it would cease to exist, and the very thought terrifying.

But as time went on and turmoil continued to reign in the garden, a different emotion began to stir within Guilt—an unfamiliar sensation: survival's guilt. It wondered if its passive stance was contributing to the ongoing chaos, and whether it could find a way to help without sacrificing its own existence.

The intensity of this newfound emotion overwhelmed Guilt. Unlike Shame and Fear, it no longer wanted to be complicit in causing harm to the garden's inhabitants. In an act driven by self-preservation and the desire to prevent further harm, Guilt chose to seal itself beside the jars of Shame and Fear, as if it were imprisoning itself as it carried the same misdemeanors with them.

Guilt couldn't help but notice the transformation occurring within Daystar. Half of Daystar's body was shrouded in the suffocating red that Shame had cast upon extending up to half of Daystar's legs. Fear's chaotic influence had added a sinister black hue to the other half. And as Guilt watched, a delicate shade of violet began to creep up Daystar's feet, an entirely new color.

This peculiar fusion of emotions left Daystar in a state of inner turmoil. Daystar felt the weight of Shame's judgment, the frenzy of Fear's chaos, and now Guilt's undeniable remorse. However, amidst this tumultuous inner struggle Daystar's excitement overflowed at the successful opening of all three jars, clearing the path for their next objective: the unleashing of destruction upon the garden.

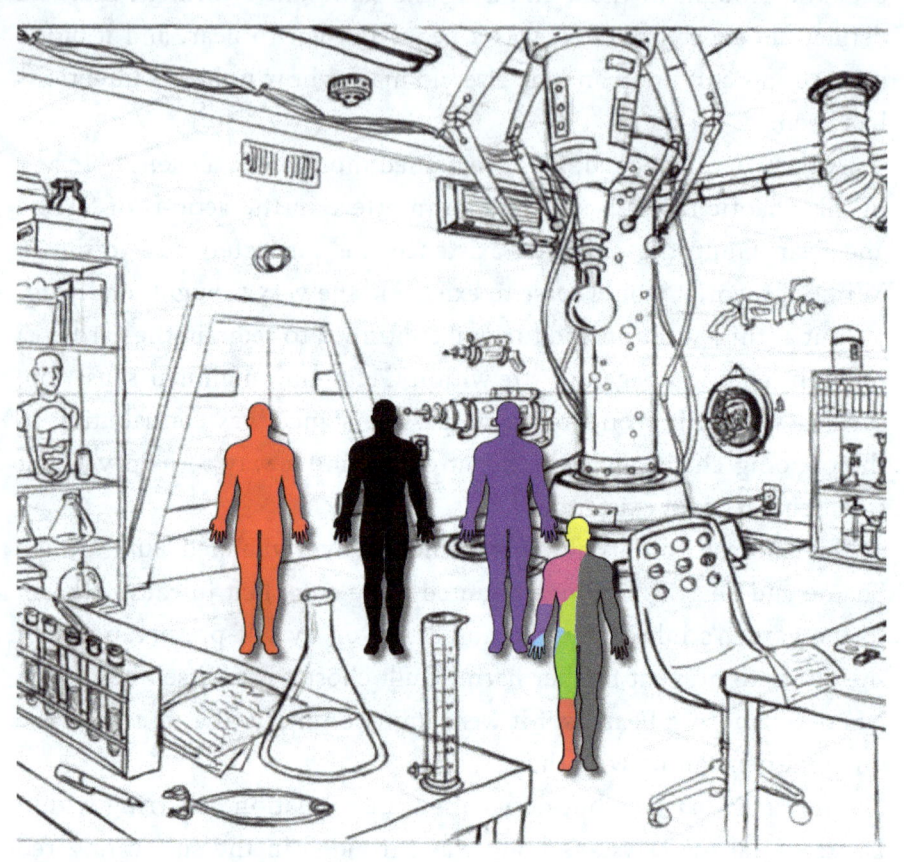

5

THE LAB

As Shame gazed upon the garden, which had once epitomized tranquility and beauty, it couldn't help but feel a rush of profound realizations coursing through it. While initially unsettling, the chaos it had unwittingly unleashed upon the inhabitants had ignited an unexpected sense of awe within Shame. It began to see the immense power in the turbulence that it had incited.

With each passing moment, Shame found itself absorbing the profound impact of its actions on this once-harmonious haven. It was as if Shame had unlocked a hidden reservoir of potential, a wellspring of transformation that had long been dormant. The garden's deterioration was a reflection of Shame's destructive tendencies and a canvas upon which it could paint the limitless facets of human experience.

Shame realized that its influence had no boundaries, no constraints. It could touch the core of human emotions and relationships, sculpting them into forms Shame had never imagined possible. The trust that had been shattered was not a testament to its hatred but a testament to the profound impact it held over the human psyche.

In this newfound awareness, Shame marveled at the garden's transformation. It was no longer a place of serenity but a realm with potential for growth and renewal. The bonds that had been fractured were not irrevocably broken; they were threads waiting to be rewoven into a tapestry of resilience and strength.

With each tear that fell, Shame recognized the opportunity for healing and redemption. It wasn't about perpetuating suffering but guiding the inhabitants towards self-discovery and empathy. The chaos was not a source of sadistic pleasure but a catalyst for profound change. Shame couldn't help but stand in awe of what it saw. The limitations it once believed existed were shattered, and it began to grasp the depth of its influence on the human experience.

Realizations began to creep into Fear's consciousness like shadows cast by a flickering flame. Amid this chaos, the garden crumbled under the weight of its influence, it couldn't help but acknowledge the potency of fear.

Fear was more than just a tool for destruction; it was a force that shaped realities and revealed the fragility of existence. It was as though the very essence of the inhabitants' existence was being reshaped by the fear that Fear had sown.

As the garden inhabitants grappled with their newfound anxieties, Fear couldn't help but become more self-aware. Any boundaries or limitations did not confine the tendrils of fear it had unleashed. They seeped into every corner of their minds, fracturing their once-peaceful existence.

The realization that fear had no constraints and could penetrate and manipulate perceptions was a chilling revelation. Fear reminded itself of its boundless power—the power to warp reality.

It found itself in awe, not of the beauty of creation, but of the sheer capacity of fear to shatter all that was once tranquil. It was a power that knew no compassion, no mercy, and as Fear gazed upon the wreckage of the garden, it knew that its journey into the depths of fear was far from over.

Amidst the chaos, a series of realizations began to flood Guilt's consciousness. Guilt had always perceived itself as a harbinger of accountability, but now, it saw the power within itself, even in this turbulent moment.

Guilt absorbed the impact of its presence on the garden, feeling it ripple through every flower and blade of grass. The pain and suffering were undeniable, but there was something profound in the experience. It could sense individuals grappling with their actions, wrestling with their conscience, and striving to rectify their mistakes. It was a raw and unfiltered manifestation of human nature, and in its way, it was powerful.

As it witnessed this chaos, Guilt realized its influence wasn't limited to merely sowing seeds of remorse. The power it witnessed was a double-edged sword, capable of inflicting wounds as deep as the healing it could inspire. The destruction and suffering were real, and it couldn't ignore the pain it caused. This was not what Guilt had intended, and it pained it deeply to see the havoc wreaked upon the sanctuary it had once known.

Its purpose had never been to contribute to this madness, to see the inhabitants suffer in this way. It had always been the reminder of one's conscience, urging them to take responsibility for their actions and make amends. But now, Guilt's influence was a twisted and perverted force that tore apart friendships and fueled anxiety.

Guilt couldn't help but share their sadness as tears filled their eyes. A profound regret coursed through Guilt, for it had never intended to lead them down this dark path. Daystar's actions had unleashed something that should have never been awakened, and it grieved for the innocence lost and the bonds shattered.

Guilt was unlike Shame and Fear, reveling in the chaos and destruction. Instead, it was burdened by the weight of the remorse it had instilled in them. It yearned for the garden to return to its former state of peace and tranquility, where its presence was a gentle nudge toward self-improvement rather than a source of torment.

Look what 'Daystar had unleashed. It was astounding. One could hardly believe the potential that was tapped into by harnessing these emotions, twisting them into something even more powerful than anyone ever imagined.

Daystar was ignorant of all this potential, the ability to manipulate the essence of Shame, Fear, and Guilt. The garden was just a canvas and Daystar had become the artist of nightmares.

Standing there reveling in the chaos, Daystar was wondering what to do next. The possibilities were as vast and dark as the void itself. It was impossible not to feel the weight of the inhabitants' suffering, their bewilderment at the sudden upheaval of their lives. It was exhilarating.

"I kinda like this," he muttered, a wicked grin curling my lips. Their pain was a sweet nectar to his senses, a reminder of the dominion over their souls. The power that was discovered to manipulate their deepest fears—it was intoxicating.

But what came next? That was the tantalizing question that danced through the mind. The garden was just the beginning, a mere taste of what could be done. What else could be done with this power? What other realms could be plunged into chaos and despair? The possibilities were as endless as the darkness that enveloped this once-peaceful sanctuary. There was an eagerness to explore them all, to push the boundaries of fear to the limits and beyond.

6

THE EMOTIONAL PANDEMIC

Once a haven of safety, this location was about to transform into a nightmare. Daystar stood in the middle of the garden, surrounded by the emotions of shame, fear, and guilt, dangerous energy coursed through Daystar's veins, fueling his destructive and chaotic thoughts.

The previously vibrant colors of the garden's plants and creatures had faded to a sickly, lifeless color. Overwhelmed by their guilt, the once proud trees bent to the ground, and the color of their leaves faded to black as they died. Once a symbol of happiness and life, flowers hung their heads in shame as a palpable feeling of humiliation existed.

Once-visible paths through the garden became deadly mazes as if an obnoxious mist were whispering its darkest secrets. Shadows created by the contorted trees were unsettling, and the ground was littered with roots that threatened to trip any passersby. As inhabitants tried to escape the repercussions of these three emotions, the garden became a labyrinth of distrust and uncertainty.

The dark and unclean waters of the garden's streams reflected the guilt of the garden's inhabitants. Once calm streams had transformed into raging rivers, their churning waters echoed the guests' emotional turmoil. The animals' mournful cries, which reverberated down the abyss, may have indicated that they, too, were burdened by guilt.

Perhaps the most striking transformation was the near absence of life. The once-bustling garden had fallen eerily silent. Birds that had once filled the air with melodious songs were gone, their absence leaving a haunting silence. The vibrant wildlife had dwindled, replaced by the hollow echoes of their former existence.

The effects of Guilt, Shame, and Fear was so pervasive that even the garden's landscape had changed. The once-calm meadows were now inaccessible and ominous due to increased thorns and brambles. Still as glass, the lakes and ponds reflected the twisted and deformed outlines of the trees around them.

Shame made its presence felt first. It entered people's minds and caused them to doubt their deeds and values. People started avoiding one another's gaze out of apprehension of being judged. They were paralyzed by worry that their secrets might be revealed. Daystar recognized an opening in this climate of uncertainty and skepticism.

Daystar saw Shame's potential to control the inhabitants and decided to partner with the emotion. They worked together to develop techniques for making people feel even worse about themselves. They quietly fueled rumors and public shaming, ensuring that none felt safe from another's' scrutiny. Daystar and Shame collaborated together and the results were devastating and felt everywhere.

Shame started by figuring out where people were weak in society. Daystar and Shame conspired, listened in on talks, and watched interactions between people, intently searching for openings to exploit.

Shame quietly injected uncertainty into their thoughts once they identified possible targets. They had a system of informants and spies that spread tales about people to make people suspicious of each other and their motives. The seeds of regret were planted, and people began to evaluate their behavior and goals.

Daystar and Shame were aware of the impact that public shaming had. Shame fostered resentment and the sharing of damaging secrets, leading to an environment where nobody felt secure sharing anything with anyone. The Inhabitants' already profound feelings of Shame were only exacerbated by the prevalence of false allegations and embarrassing exposés.

But Shame was not the only emotion Daystar sought to exploit. Fear was just as effective, and Daystar realized that by playing on people's fears, they could have even more control over their behavior. The uncertainty of what would happen next paralyzed them. Daystar collaborated with Fear to manipulate people's thoughts and behaviors. They worked in tandem to convey the fear of imminent disasters and hidden dangers. People's willingness to accept Daystar's instructions increased as their dread of the world around them grew.

Fear recognized that uncertainty was a powerful breeding ground for fear. It used subtle manipulation tactics to create an atmosphere of insecurity in society. Ambiguity and unanswered questions became the norm, leaving people anxious and on edge.

Fear spread rumors of impending disasters and unseen threats. These rumors were carefully crafted to tap into people's deepest fears —from natural disasters to imagined conspiracies. These whispers of impending doom only served to heighten the pervasiveness of fear.

Fear and Daystart worked hard to create an environment where everyone felt vulnerable. They portrayed fear as a motivator for survival, urging people to take drastic measures to protect themselves and their loved ones. This further solidified Daystar's influence over society.

And then there was Guilt, the most insidious of all. Guilt weighed heavily on people's hearts, making them question their actions. Daystar recognized the power of Guilt to control and manipulate, and was quick to create a strategic plan to wreak havoc on the inhabitants. Together, they pushed individuals to make choices that would ultimately lead to feelings of guilt and regret. People were torn between their desires and moral compass, and Daystar reveled in their inner turmoil.

They understood that guilt often arises from moral dilemmas, so they strategically introduced situations where individuals had to choose between conflicting values. These situations were designed to be emotionally charged, forcing people to make difficult decisions that they would regret.

Daystar subtly encouraged self-interest over altruism. Guilt made individuals second-guess their decisions. They highlighted the potential consequences of each choice, emphasizing the negative outcomes resulting from following their desires. This constant focus on regret eroded people's confidence in their choices.

As the emotions of Shame, Fear, and Guilt continued to cascade through the garden, they began to work in tandem with one another. People felt ashamed of their fears and guilty about succumbing to them. They were trapped in a never-ending cycle of self-recrimination, unable to break free from the grip of these powerful emotions.

Judgments became harsher, perspectives became narrower, and these emotions overwhelmed and influenced twisted desires. Collaboration between the emotions was seamless, as they fed off each other's energy, creating a self-sustaining cycle of misery and despair.

Daystar watched with satisfaction as their plan unfolded. The emotions of Shame, Fear, and Guilt had proven to be remarkably effective tools for manipulation. Inhabitants had become a puppet in their hands and Daystar's influence over the world was stronger than ever.

Daystar couldn't help but wonder if they were unleashing forces beyond their control. The world was descending into chaos, and Daystar couldn't help but question whether they had made a grave mistake in controlling the obtained power.

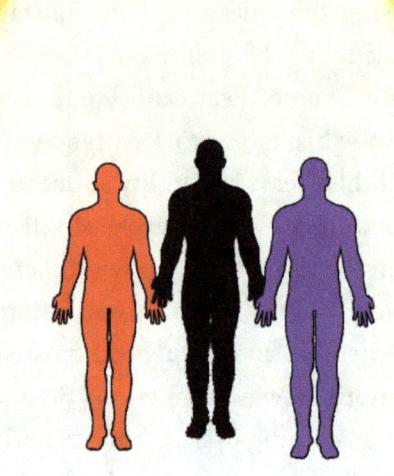

7

THE ENLIGHTENMENT

Amid turmoil and despair, a change was brewing beneath the world's surface. The Source, the enigmatic entity that initiated the imprisonment of Shame, Fear and Guilt sensed that it was time to return and give the inhabitants the tools they need to create a balance in the garden.

One day, as the sun hung low on the horizon, casting long shadows across the land, the Source reappeared, commanding the attention of all who beheld it. The inhabitants burdened by the heavy chains of their emotions, watched in awe as the Source materialized before them once more.

In a voice that resonated with wisdom and compassion, the Source began to speak. "My dear inhabitants, I have returned to offer you a revelation. It is time to cast aside the shackles that bind you to the emotions of Shame, Fear, and Guilt. They are not your masters but facets of your inner world, mirrors reflecting your experiences."

A collective gasp swept through the crowd, their eyes filled with wonder and curiosity.

The Source continued. "You have given these emotions power by allowing them to dictate your actions and rule your lives. But know this: you can have a different relationship with them. You can acknowledge their existence, embrace their lessons, and transform them into allies rather than adversaries."

The people exchanged glances, the weight of this revelation sinking in. It was like a veil had been lifted, revealing a new way of perceiving their emotions.

"You do not have to obey Shame, Fear, or Guilt," the Source proclaimed. "You have bestowed upon them their dominion over your lives. It is through your fear and avoidance that they have gained their power. But the choice to change that relationship is yours to make."

A sense of empowerment began to ripple through the crowd. The notion that they held the key to liberation from these emotions sparked a newfound hope.

"Consider a time when you felt Shame for a past action. Perhaps you wronged someone or made a mistake. In that moment of Shame, you acknowledged your capacity for empathy and compassion. Shame was your conscience, guiding you toward making amends and becoming a better person."

"Think about the times when Fear was your friend and not your foe. Fear was your guardian, cautioning you to be mindful of potential dangers. It encouraged you to evaluate risks and make informed choices. It is not an enemy but a companion of self-preservation."

"Recall moments when Guilt weighed heavily upon your heart. Guilt was your moral compass, reminding you of your values and principles. It prompted you to reflect on your actions and consider the consequences. Embracing Guilt allowed you to realign your choices with your beliefs."

The Source's voice softened, conveying guidance and understanding. "Shame, Fear, and Guilt are not malevolent forces. They are what you choose to make them. They are messengers, bringing insights about your inner world. They reveal your values, your vulnerabilities, and your growth potential. To have a relationship with them is to embark on a journey of self-discovery."

With this newfound strength and insight, the inhabitants began to forge a deeper connection with their emotions. They realized that they alone held the power over their lives, and the goal was not to rid themselves of these emotions but to holistically address them. They understood that shame could coexist with self-compassion, fear could be a catalyst for personal growth, and guilt could guide them toward alignment with their values. This epiphany marked a turning point in their journey, as they embarked on a path of embracing their emotions and using them as tools for self-discovery and transformation.

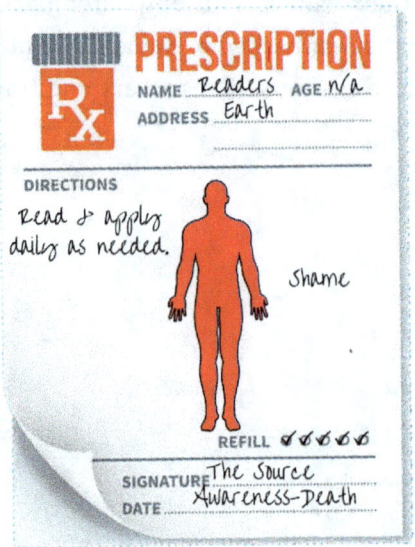

8

PRESCRIPTION FOR SHAME

In the heart of the garden, a hidden struggle had ensnared the inhabitants. They were entangled in the suffocating embrace of shame, a burden they carried as they covered themselves behind the trees. Each tree was a symbol of their past transgressions, their regrets, and their perceived inadequacies.

The people who resided in this garden felt shame for various reasons. Some felt shame for the hurt they had caused others, the wounds they had inflicted through their thoughtless words and actions. Others felt shame for their mistakes, the wrong turns they had taken on their life's journey, and the missed opportunities. Many carried the weight of societal expectations, feeling shame for not living up to the standards imposed upon them.

As the days passed, the memory of the Source's words echoed in their minds.

"Consider a time when you felt shame for a past action, in that moment of shame, you acknowledged the realities of imperfections and embraced the capacity for empathy and compassion. Shame made you more conscious, guiding you towards improvement and becoming a better person."

This reflection planted a seed of realization within them. Shame, they understood, was not a malevolent force seeking to punish them; it was a teacher, a guide on the path of self-improvement. Shame reminded them of their capacity to feel empathy, to acknowledge their mistakes, and to strive for a better future.

With this new understanding, a transformation began to stir among the inhabitants. They no longer wanted to hide behind the trees, for they recognized that doing so only perpetuated the cycle of shame. Instead, they yearned to reveal the truth about themselves, to confront the reality of their emotions directly.

One by one, they approached the grove of trees that had concealed them for so long. Their hearts raced with trepidation, but determination shone in their eyes. They knew that taking down the covers symbolized their commitment to face their emotions, especially shame, without avoidance or denial.

As the inhabitants worked together to remove the branches and shadows, a sense of realization washed over them. The importance of shame became clear to them. It was a mirror reflecting their values, vulnerabilities, and growth potential. By embracing it, they could harness its power as a catalyst for positive change, a reminder to make amends and a guide toward becoming better versions of themselves.

They recognized that shame often rooted itself in past actions or circumstances, but its true power was felt in the present moment. The way they responded to shame, the decisions they made in its presence, and the self-compassion they practiced all happened in the present.

The similarities between the present and shame became increasingly apparent. Just as the present was a fleeting and ever-changing moment, so was the experience of shame. It ebbed and flowed like the passing of time, reminding them that it was a transient emotion, not a permanent state of being. The inhabitants realized that, much like the present, shame required their attention and acceptance in the now.

One by one, they responded to the judgmental comments and whispers. They spoke about how they had already acknowledged their past mistakes and were actively working to make amends and become better versions of themselves. They acknowledged that shame was a natural part of the process but emphasized that it was not meant to be a tool for condemnation.

Their heartfelt responses began to shift the atmosphere in the gathering. Some in the crowd started empathizing, realizing they had made mistakes and carried their shame. The negative energy dissipated as understanding and compassion took its place.

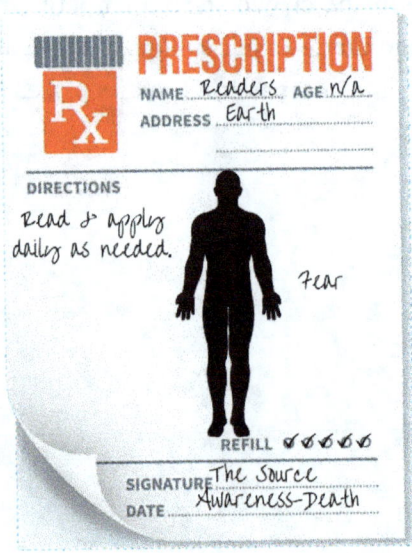

9

PRESCRIPTION FOR FEAR

The garden inhabitants had lived in blissful ignorance for as long as they could remember. Their days were filled with vibrant colors, fragrant blossoms, and gentle leaves rustling. But now, a cloud of fear had descended upon them, shrouding their paradise in darkness.

They felt fear in the pit of their stomachs, a gnawing uncertainty that left them trembling and disoriented. Fear had crept into their once-tranquil garden, and it seemed to be everywhere. Fear of the unknown, fear of change, fear of each other. The inhabitants had retreated to the darkest corners of the garden, seeking refuge from the ever-present menace.

As they huddled together in the inky blackness, fear began to play tricks on their minds. Hallucinations danced before their eyes like malevolent specters. Whispers of imaginary tornadoes swept through their thoughts, conjuring images of swirling winds and chaos. They saw disasters unfold, mountains crumbling, and rivers running dry. Unseen threats lurked in the shadows, like monsters ready to pounce.

Their collective paranoia deepened, and they clung to one another, their hearts racing. Each hallucination intensified their terror, and the once-lush garden felt like a nightmarish landscape.

Fear, they understood, often took root in concerns about what might happen in the days and years ahead. It was a reaction to the uncertainty of the future, a response to the unknown and its potential dangers.

The similarities between the future and fear became increasingly apparent. Just as fear was a natural response to anticipating what lay ahead, the future was defined by uncertainty and unpredictability. Both fear and the future existed in the realm of possibilities, where the imagination could run wild with positive and negative scenarios.

But amid this darkness, a faint memory stirred within them. It was the voice of the Source, echoing in their minds, reminding them of a time when fear had been their guardian, not their tormentor. The Source's words reverberated through their thoughts.

"Think about the times when fear was your friend and not your foe. Fear was your guardian, cautioning you to be mindful of potential dangers. It encouraged you to evaluate risks and make informed choices. It is not an enemy but a companion of self-preservation."

As these words resurfaced, a glimmer of understanding began to dawn upon the inhabitants. They realized that the hallucinations, born from their unfounded fears, were creations of their minds. Fear distorted their perception of reality, making them see threats where none existed.

Slowly, they started to calm themselves, holding onto the knowledge that fear was not the enemy but a natural response to the unknown. They whispered words of reassurance to one another, reminding themselves they were in control of their thoughts and emotions.

One by one, the hallucinations faded, dissipating like wisps of smoke. Though still shrouded in darkness, the garden no longer felt like a nightmarish realm. The inhabitants realized they had the power to mitigate the effects of fear and to distinguish between genuine threats and irrational anxieties.

In a symbolic gesture, they shed the shrouds that had hidden them in obscurity. It was not an endeavor to banish apprehension but a proclamation that they were prepared to step into the limelight to confront their anxieties head-on. They understood that fear would never truly vanish, yet they could coexist with it, temper its influence, and harness it as a personal development and self-preservation tool.

The garden was once again bathed in the warm, welcoming radiance as the coverings dissolved. The inhabitants exchanged knowing glances, now equipped with a newfound comprehension. Fear had imparted a valuable lesson—it was not a foe to be vanquished but a companion to be embraced. Armed with this wisdom, they ventured forth on their ongoing odyssey through the ever-evolving terrain of their garden, fully aware that fear would be there, guiding them along the path of self-preservation and growth.

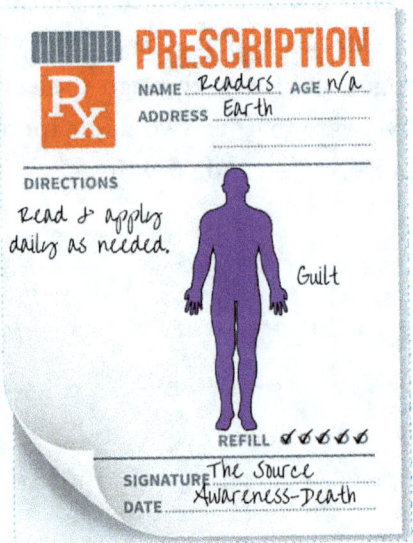

10

PRESCRIPTION FOR GUILT

The inhabitants of the garden found themselves entangled in a web of guilt. It clung to them like a heavy cloak, weighing down their hearts and clouding their once-harmonious relationships. They were overcompensating with each other, their actions driven by an overwhelming need to alleviate their sense of wrongdoing.

Guilt had permeated their lives, casting shadows on their idyllic existence. It manifested in countless ways. Some felt guilt for taking more than their fair share of resources, while others were burdened by the knowledge that they had not done enough to help their fellow inhabitants. Every interaction, every decision, seemed tainted by this suffocating emotion.

Just as the past was unchangeable, immutable, and forever etched into their history, so too was guilt an indelible mark on their conscience. Both had the power to cast long shadows over their lives, reminding them of their deeds and decisions.

The past served as a repository of lessons learned, a source of wisdom that could guide their future choices. Guilt, in its way, played a similar role. It was a relentless teacher, reminding them of their values and principles and prompting them to reflect on their actions and consider the consequences.

One scenario that had left a deep mark on their collective conscience was a dispute over a particularly bountiful harvest. When the garden had yielded an abundance of fruits, some inhabitants had claimed a disproportionate share, leaving others with less than they needed.

Tensions had been simmering for days, with murmurs of discontent spreading like wildfire through the garden. As the dispute escalated, it culminated in a dramatic showdown beneath the shade of the ancient oak tree. Inhabitants, their faces contorted with anger and frustration, gathered in a heated circle, their voices raised in a cacophony of accusations and grievances.

The guilt had gnawed at the hearts of those who had taken more, knowing that they had caused suffering to their neighbors.

Amid this emotional turmoil, the inhabitants began to recall the wisdom of the Source's words. "Recall moments when Guilt weighed heavily upon your heart. Guilt was your moral compass, reminding you of your values and principles. It prompted you to reflect on your actions and consider the consequences. Embracing Guilt allowed you to realign your choices with your beliefs."

These words stirred something within them, a realization that guilt was not an enemy to be avoided but a powerful tool for self-reflection and moral growth. They understood guilt was their inner compass, guiding them back to the path of their shared values and principles.

With this newfound perspective, they paused in their relentless quest to overcompensate for their perceived wrongs. They saw that their actions, driven by guilt, were sometimes excessive and disproportionate. Instead of healing their relationships, they had inadvertently strained them further.

The importance of guilt became clearer to them. It was not meant to paralyze them with remorse but to encourage self-awareness and accountability. Guilt, when harnessed wisely, could lead to positive change and reconciliation.

Slowly, the inhabitants began approaching their relationships and decisions with a more balanced perspective. They acknowledged their past mistakes and made amends where necessary, but they also learned to forgive themselves. They understood guilt was not a burden to be carried indefinitely but a reminder to strive for better.

As the weight of excessive guilt lifted, the garden regained some of its former tranquility. The inhabitants worked together, not out of fear of guilt but of a shared commitment to their values. They learned that guilt, when tempered with understanding and self-compassion, could guide their journey toward a more harmonious and principled existence.

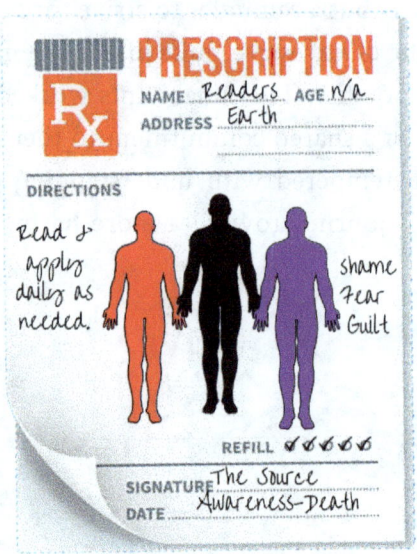

11

PRESCRIPTIONS FOR THE TRIUMVIRATE

As the garden inhabitants continued their journey, they made steady progress in learning to embrace shame, fear, and guilt individually. These emotions had unique lessons to offer, and the inhabitants were beginning to understand their importance.

Shame, for instance, had taught them about self-compassion. Some inhabitants had begun to accept their flaws and mistakes with kindness rather than self-condemnation. They understood that it was human to err, and by acknowledging their shame, they could pave the way for growth and change.

Fear encouraged them to be cautious but pushed them to confront their anxieties. They realized that facing their fears head-on often led to personal growth and resilience. Fear was no longer seen as an obstacle but a challenge to overcome.

Guilt was a moral compass, guiding them toward accountability and self-reflection. It prompted them to make amends when necessary and to align their actions with their values. When harnessed wisely, the inhabitants learned that guilt could lead to positive change and reconciliation.

The Triumvirate, consisting of Shame, Fear, and Guilt, watched with a growing sense of disappointment as the garden inhabitants attempted to embrace these emotions individually. To them, the inhabitants' efforts felt misguided and frustratingly inadequate.

The Triumvirate had long held sway over the inhabitants, guiding them in their actions and decisions. However, witnessing the inhabitants' shift towards confronting, acknowledging, and reconciling with these emotions left Shame, Fear, and Guilt disheartened. They couldn't comprehend why the inhabitants chose a path that seemed counter to their purpose.

Determined to address the inhabitants and make them understand their perspective, the Triumvirate decided to present themselves to the inhabitants as one. They knew that it was time to intervene and demonstrate that the prescriptions the inhabitants had been following to face shame, fear, and guilt were insufficient when dealing with the three of them together.

Daystar, who had initially unleashed Shame, Fear, and Guilt upon the garden, reappeared in their midst. Turning to the Triumvirate—Shame, Fear, and Guilt—Daystar proposed an unexpected alliance. "It is time for these emotions to reveal their full power, to remind you of the depths of their influence. Together, they shall show you the complexity of their interplay."

The Triumvirate nodded in agreement, and with a synchronized effort, they began to weave a potent tapestry of emotions. Shame whispered into the inhabitants' ears, reminding them of past mistakes and flaws. Fear gripped their hearts, causing them to tremble with uncertainty. Guilt weighed heavily upon their shoulders, urging them to overcompensate for their perceived wrongs.

The inhabitants felt a surge of fear, overcompensation, and shame like never before. It was an overwhelming experience, and they struggled to find their footing in the face of this powerful onslaught.

As Shame, Fear, and Guilt faded away, they left the inhabitants with a profound question lingering in the air, "What are we going to do now?" It was a question that hung heavy in their hearts, urging them to reconsider their approach to these powerful emotions and to find a way to navigate the intricate dance of shame, fear, and guilt as a harmonious trio.

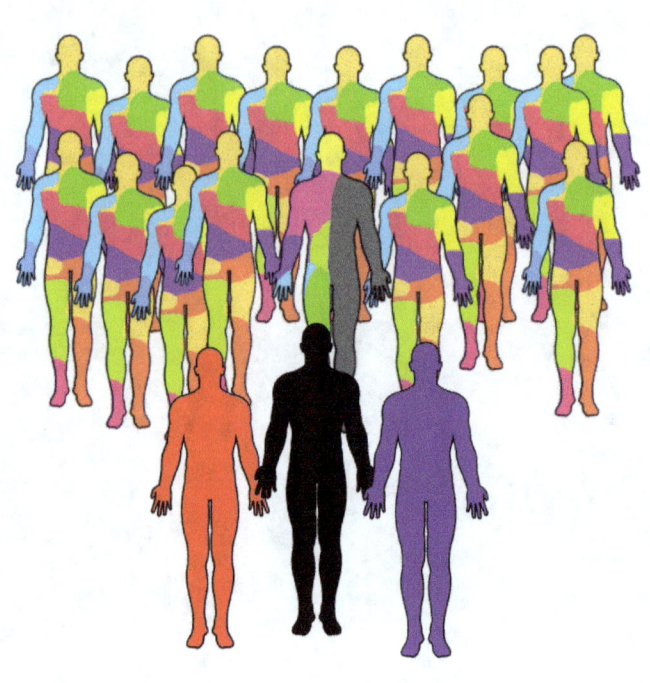

12

SYMBIOSIS

One day, a group of inhabitants found themselves grappling with overwhelming fear as they prepared to embark on a daring project that had the potential for great success but was also uncertain. The fear was palpable, casting a shadow over their enthusiasm.

Just as they gathered to discuss their concerns, Shame, Fear and Guilt made their presence known. They whispered to the fearful inhabitants.

"You're setting yourselves up for failure. Look at how fear has gripped you. How can you possibly succeed when you're paralyzed by it?"

The inhabitants felt a wave of shame wash over them, their confidence waning. They began to question their abilities and the wisdom of their decisions. Guilt chimed in, "Perhaps you should reconsider for the sake of your peace of mind. Is it worth risking your sense of self-worth for this endeavor?"

As a different group of inhabitants found themselves wrestling with deep-seated shame, they applied the prescription they had learned. They began to acknowledge their shame, confront it, and take steps towards self-compassion and self-forgiveness.

However, Fear and Guilt, who had witnessed this attempt to address shame, couldn't stand idly by. They approached the inhabitants who were trying to work through their shame.

Fear whispered with urgency, "You're deluding yourselves into thinking you can overcome shame. It's a part of you, ingrained deep within. You'll never be free from it."

Guilt added, "You should remember your mistakes and failures. How can you move forward without your shame guiding you?"

Fear, shame, and guilt were working in unison, amplifying the doubts and insecurities of the inhabitants.

But then, a voice emerged from the shadows—a voice of reason and resilience. An inhabitant, who had previously experienced this trio's tactics, stepped forward.

"You may be right," the inhabitant conceded, addressing Shame, Fear, and Guilt. "Fear has a strong grip on us, and it's natural to feel vulnerable. But we've learned something crucial on our journey—that these emotions are not our enemies, but rather, they're part of the tapestry of our humanity. They challenge us but remind us that we're pushing boundaries, taking risks, and striving for growth."

The other inhabitants nodded in agreement, their collective strength building. "We understand that fear, shame, and guilt are here to guide us, not to deter us. We've learned to acknowledge our fears, confront our shame, and take responsibility for our actions. In doing so, we gain wisdom, resilience, and the capacity to make informed choices."

Shame, Fear, and Guilt listened, intrigued by this newfound resolve. They had expected to sow doubt and hesitation, but instead, they witnessed the inhabitants harnessing their emotions for strength.

The inhabitant said, "You see, we can uncover and unhide shame and fear simultaneously. We don't have to choose one over the other. We can move forward with authenticity and courage by accepting our imperfections and confronting our fears."

"You know," they began, their voice steady and confident, "we've learned that it's not necessary to overcompensate or hide our fear of not being understood. We've discovered that we can control our thoughts and reactions. We don't need to be slaves to our anxieties or insecurities."

Another inhabitant nodded in agreement, continuing the thought, "The prescription for fear and guilt works when we recognize that we can choose to confront our fears, acknowledge our guilt, and move forward with intention. We don't need to be paralyzed by these emotions; instead, we can use them as stepping stones to personal growth and self-discovery."

As the inhabitants continued to share their realization of dealing with shame, fear, and guilt collectively, the Triumvirate couldn't help but be taken aback. They were shocked that the inhabitants had found a way to navigate these three powerful emotions together harmoniously.

Day by day, the inhabitants grew accustomed to the constant companionship of Shame, Fear, and Guilt. They no longer fought against their presence, realizing that these emotions, though formidable, were an integral part of the human experience.

And so, with unwavering determination and the support of their community, the inhabitants had rewritten the narrative of their lives. Together, they stood as living proof that even the most formidable emotions could be conquered, as long as they faced them with courage, empathy, and a shared resolve to triumph over adversity.

Shame, Fear, and Guilt live in perpetuity, always watching. They dwell in the shadows, concealed within the very essence of the community. They lurk in the tall grasses of the garden, whispering in the swaying trees, or masking themselves amidst the vibrant colors of the blooming flowers. They remained an ever-present mystery, a constant reminder of the need for self-awareness. The Triumvirate are three relentless companions always on the prowl for old or new inhabitants yet to be awakened to their presence. And all of this reminds us that the journey of self-awareness is one that never truly ends.

13

APPENDIX I

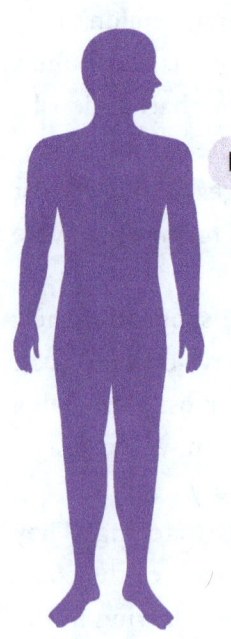

PAST Emotion

Performance Based Emotion

GUILT

I am uniquely related to your past self. I perceive life as coming against me. I am processed by your intuition. I present myself as one who is grounded. The primary ways people manage ME are by using power, peace and principles. My primary question for you and others is **HOW AM I DOING?**

14

APPENDIX II

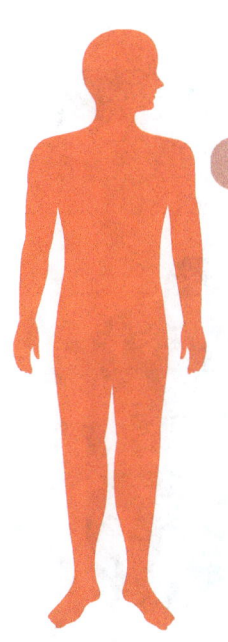

PRESENT Emotion

Identity Based Emotion

SHAME

I am uniquely related to your present self. I perceive life as an opportunity to connect with others. I am processed by your feelings. I present myself relationally. The primary ways people manage ME are by serving, succeeding and being special. My primary question for you and others is **WHO AM I?**

15

APPENDIX III

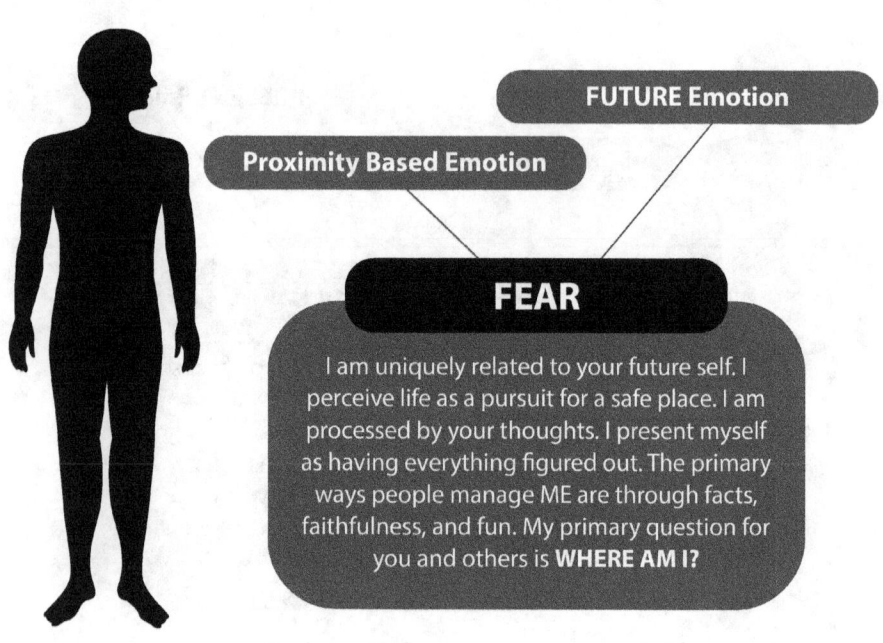

ABOUT THE AUTHOR

Michael is a serial intellectual. He creates intellectual products that transform people and change the world. He was born in Los Angeles and lived there for almost four decades. In 2009, he moved to Baltimore City and has lived there for fourteen years. Michael has five beautiful adult children. Michael has a bachelor's degree in political studies with an emphasis in philosophy as well as a master's degree in divinity.

He is a certified Enneagram administrator, Scrum master and trained in project management. Michael has been coaching and consulting for twenty-five years. He has founded and led multiple nonprofit organizations. Michael is the author of ten books; 100 Meditations: An Everyday Book for Everyday People; Don't Plant, Be Planted; Metamorphic Dictis; Be You; Social Revolution is Baltimore's Only Solution, Hard Questions, Tenses, Differentiated and Limitations and Loses . Michael is also the creator of many personal development tools: Pause exercise, Emotional MRI, and How to Write Strategic Affirmations, The Pillars of Personal Development, The Priority Funnel, Quadrascope, Mirror Exercise and the Life Map.

Michael is an accomplished triathlete and has completed all four distances. Michael's favorite sport is motocross, his favorite fast food is In-N-Out Burger, he is addicted to fresh Reese's Peanut Butter Cups, and absolutely loves rottweilers. His favorite animals are killer whales and tigers. One of his favorite authors is Mark Twain, and one of his favorite quotes from him is "The two most important days of your life are the day you are born and the day you find out why."

www.ingramcontent.com/pod-product-compliance
Lightning Source LLC
Chambersburg PA
CBHW070440010526
44118CB00014B/2125